Remember the King

Mike Abrahamian

ISBN 978-0-6151-5143-4

Published by Sivle Books
P.O. Box 41
Burbank, Ca 91503

I would like to thank everyone who supported me during the making of this book. It would not have been possible without your support. A special thanks to my beautiful fiancée Krista, I love you baby.

Dedicated to the memories of Elvis, Gladys, Vernon and Jessie

Table of Contents

Introduction

These poems are my way of trying to give back to a man who gave so much of himself to so many people. For me, Elvis was so much more than an entertainer. He was a kind and loving person, who loved to share his time and success with all who surrounded him and those who he had never met. It's almost impossible to describe him with a few words, but I hope that these poems give you a better understanding of who he was as a person. To those who share my feelings, I hope these poems reflect the feelings you carry in your heart.

"I don't feel that I'll live a long life. That's why I've got to get what I can out of everyday." -Elvis

Ever lasting love that your fans have...
Loyalty that we show every year at Graceland...
Voice that shakes us to our foundation...
Inspiration that you give us through your songs...
Soul that you shared with millions until the end...

Perfection that you wanted in your music...
Religion that you loved and had faith in...
Every fan loves you more than you know...
Style that you had never to be duplicated...
Love you gave to everyone around...
Education you gave that we still haven't found...
Your music lives on and will for all time.

5-10-07

"He was as big as the whole country itself, as big as the whole dream. He just embodied the essence of it and he was in mortal combat with the thing. Nothing will ever take the place of that guy." -Bruce Springsteen

Journeyed into heaven, an angel with wings...
Elvis loved him till the very end...
Sweet angel that never had a chance...
Singled out by God for an angelic task...
Intended for earth and went to heaven...
Elvis saw him every time he looked in a mirror...

Gave his life to his brother...
Arrived in heaven too soon...
Remembered for all time...
On Elvis' mind everyday...
Never to be forgotten by Elvis.

"Elvis never seemed the same once his mother passed. He loved her more than anything." -Anonymous

Gave her love to her son every moment of her life...
Loved her son more than words can describe...
Admired her son for becoming a man...
Devoted to Elvis till her very last breath...
Youthful in spirit taken away far too soon...
Simple yet elegant in her own beautiful way.

Loved her son till the very end...
Opened her heart for the world to see...
Vital part of Elvis' life...
Ever lasting devotion to her son.

"It's rare when an artist's talent can touch an entire generation of people. It's even rarer when that same influence affects several generations. Elvis made an imprint on the world of pop music unequaled by any other single performer." -Dick Clark

Although we'll never know what happened on that night...
His fans will always love him and keep his name alive...
Even though he is gone and no longer in our sight...
His fans remain loyal and sing his songs all through the night...
Although the King is gone and no longer singing...
His music remains locked deep within our hearts.

7-16-06

"Mama I'd give back every penny and go back to digging ditches just to have you back." -Elvis

Elvis and Gladys

She may have been simple; she might have been
plain...
Through Elvis' eyes she was a beautiful queen...
He was loved and protected every step of the way...
Through Gladys' eyes he was an angel with wings...
They loved each other more than words can describe...
I think it's safe to say when she left his world, he
never felt the same...
We can feel safe knowing they're together in heaven
with Jessie and Vernon a family once again.

"None of us could have made it without Elvis."
-Buddy Holly

Elvis and Lisa

Although he was gone before she could say goodbye...
He loved her more than words can describe...
Even though she was young and innocent inside...
She lost her loving father without knowing why...
Although he's been gone for all these years...
Her heart still aches inside as she holds back all her
tears.

11-27-06

"I've been scratched and bitten, I just accept it with a broad mind, they don't intend to hurt ya, they just want pieces of ya to take home as a souvenir." -Elvis

No matter where you go or what you do, Elvis fans will always be true…

They loved him in the beginning and they loved him till the end…

We have a special bond between one another that most people don't understand…

We gather each year at the 'Castle' he called home…

To remember the good times of the man we call the King…

Although he's been gone for all these years we still look toward the sky and wonder where he is.

"Before Elvis there was nothing." -John Lennon

He may have been young and still a little shy...
He changed the world of music in the blink of an
eye...
He may have been wild and crazy at times...
He gave the world of music a fresh breath of life...
He sang to an audience like no other man...
He changed the world of music like no one else ever
had.

"Every time I think that I'm getting old and gradually going to the grave, something else happens." -Elvis

There's a special kind of bond between a son and his
mother...
No matter how big he becomes he will always love
her...
Although he was a legend to everyone around...
Gladys' always protected him until she was no longer
around...
Although she was gone and no longer there...
Elvis never stopped loving his sweet, sweet mother.

2-27-07

"God must have been impatient for some rock 'n' roll in heaven." -Jimmy Saville

Elvis' Gospel

No matter where you go or what you do...
One mans words can always comfort your fears...
From your highest high or lowest low...
The way he sings gospel will never leave your soul...
Life may seem mean and hard at times...
Just listen to his gospel to comfort your soul.

"I get lonesome right in the middle of a crowd."
-Elvis

He had everything he needed and wanted, yet he kept looking for something more…
His home became a prison and friends became guards…
His fame became a trap for those who sought money or acclaim…
His feelings were lost somewhere in a song never to be found…
Although he survived for as long as he did, half of his soul was forever lost.

"Elvis was a giant and influenced everyone in the business." -Isaac Hayes

He was the King of music to fans all over the world…
Although he made millions and had people all
around…
He had no one to trust, not even his pals…
Although he was loved and cherished by millions…
He had no one around to understand his problem's…
Although he was the biggest star on the planet…
He died of a broken heart with no one around.

"A live concert to me is exciting because of all the electricity that's generated in the crowd and on stage."
-Elvis

He came into our lives before we could blink...
Although he was here for such a short time...
We will never forget that left-sided smile...
He poured his heart out to us every time he would
sing...
In return we gave him our ever lasting loyalty...
I hope where ever he may be...
He is singing and smiling once again.

"He was an integrator, Elvis was a blessing. They wouldn't let black music through. He opened the door for black music. Thank god for Elvis Presley." -Little Richard

In the beginning, some said he was vulgar and some said he was crazy...
Looking back through all the years...
It's easy to see they never let him breathe...
Although the cameras and questions never stopped...
He always smiled and replied "yes sir"...
He had more pressure on him than I'll understand...
Which is what makes him a special kind of man.

"I've been to a lot of places but I haven't seen any of 'em really. The only part I don't like is staying away from home so much." -Elvis

He made us laugh and he made us cry...
His fans truly loved him more then he'll ever know...
No matter what was said or what we were told...
We never stopped loving the man who changed the
world...
Although he is gone from our sight...
We shall never forget the King of night.

"He's naturally kind and thoughtful and good. Best of all, in spite of his huge success -- he's unassuming."
-Connie Stevens

He may have made millions and owned lots of cars...
He never stopped giving to those most in need...
From the shirt off his back...
Or the ring from his finger...
He always kept giving without being asked...
No matter what the amount or what was being asked...
He always kept giving and never asked for anything back.

"On August 16, 1977, we not only lost the greatest entertainer the world has ever seen, but we lost a part of ourselves that we haven't been able to get back. I don't think the world has been the same since we lost Elvis. The day he left our world was the day the music died." -Mike

*Although he was a superstar and known all around
the planet...
He always remained humble and never took it for
granted...
Although he was busy and always had to go...
He always slowed down to stop and say hello...
Now that he is gone and resting there at Graceland...
I feel it's time for us to stop and say hello.*

"I don't know if I was his best friend, but he was mine." -Charlie Hodge

We went crazy every time we heard his voice...
We loved to hear that southern voice and big child-like
laugh...
He kept us entertained every time he went on stage...
We stayed until the very end and always wanted
more...
Although we won't see the likes of him anymore...
We still have the memories and hopes of meeting him
in Heaven.

"I don't sound like nobody." -Elvis

Is he the fallen hero that we should all be looking for…
Thirty years after his death people still worship him…
The one star that was not forgotten after his demise…
His legacy has survived for thirty years and will continue for many more…
Elvis had something we're all looking for yet we can't find…
What would you do with the gift he was given if you found it?

"He was ahead of his time because he had such deep feelings. He had the privilege of deep feelings because he was deeply loved by his mother, Gladys. He was able to appreciate profound beauty in sounds. And he started a musical revolution. They say all revolutions start from love." -Imelda Marcos

He loved his momma more than words can describe...
She left his world before he could say goodbye...
Although he was young and had family all around...
He dearly missed his momma and wanted her around...
Although he became the biggest star on the planet...
From the day his momma passed he never seemed the same.

"Truth is like the sun. You can shut it out for a time, but it ain't goin' away." -Elvis

He gave the world something to talk about…
He brought joy into millions of lives…
He entertained us like no one else had…
He kept rocking and rolling through the good times
and the bad…
He became the King of music and if you don't like it,
too damn bad.

"There was something just bordering on rudeness about Elvis. He never actually did anything rude, but he always seemed as if he was just going to. On a scale of one to ten, I would rate him eleven." -Sammy Davis Jr.

He sang music like no other man...
He had a style that made women cry...
He always had that special twinkle in his eye...
He had something special and boy did he shine...
He was the King from Memphis and his legend will
never die.

"Some people tap their feet, some people snap their fingers, and some people sway back and forth. I just sorta do 'em all together, I guess." -Elvis

He was the hillbilly cat from Memphis Tennessee…
He arrived in a flash and boy could he sing…
Although he dressed flashy and looked really keen…
He was the hillbilly cat and boy could he sing.

"Elvis' voice was that type of voice that agreed with a thought of cavalry. He was a bundle of energy sent to music, and that echo will never die." -Dr. W. Herbert Brewster

His fans loved to see that smile on his face...
We longed for the sound of his voice...
No matter what he said or did we couldn't stop
following him...
Every time he went on stage he gave us his best and
we gave him our love...
He will always remain in our hearts and thoughts...
The King is gone but his name and legacy lives forever.

"Elvis will always be the King no matter what."
-Fan comment June 1977

Although he was crowned the King of rock 'n roll...
To many of his fans, he was the King of so much
more...
No matter what he was doing or where he was
going...
He smiled and slowed down to stop and say hello...
He always kept giving to those most in need...
Which is why he's simply called 'The King'.

3-04-07

"My Favorite is How Great Thou Art, makes ya feel good and brings tears to your eyes." -Fan comment, June 1977

Last Farewell

Although he was hurting and in a lot of pain...
He stood there and sang, not once did he complain...
Little did we know it was his last farewell...
His fans cherished every moment and loved him like hell...
If only we had known it was his last farewell...
We might have slowed down to bid him farewell.

"His music still makes you feel good, and makes you want to move." -Anonymous

He may have only lived to the age of forty two...
He broke all the records and made some new ones
too...
Although it's been thirty years since that day...
His record's still stand to this very day...
Even though we haven't seen him for almost thirty
years...
His legacy lives on and never will that change.

2-27-07

"I have four of his gospel albums." -Fan comment,
June 1977

Never has there been another performer that sang with such feeling...
Every song that he sang came from his soul...
He had the greatest voice that we've ever heard...
No matter what time of day he could hit any note...
Every time that he sang, we lost our control...
He sang with such feeling and always let it show.

"I believe he talked to his brother Jessie from time to time." -Anonymous

Elvis and Jessie

He may have had money and people all around…
He felt something was missing and searched all
around…
He read every book that was handed on down…
Something was still missing and keeping him down…
He looked in the mirror and realized what it was…
He saw his twin brother Jessie looking down from
above.

"I think Elvis thought of Jessie throughout his life, and carried his spirit with him." -Anonymous

Jessie Garon

Although we never saw his precious little face...
I think it's safe to say his brother took his place...
He carried all the burden and carried all the pain...
Although he never knew him, he saw him everyday...
Even though he was loved and cherished by
millions...
Elvis never stopped loving his little twin brother.

"Although he bought houses in other states, Graceland was always his home." -Fan comment

The King's Tomb

Graceland has become a 20th century pyramid...
It once was a home full of life and love...
It's now filled with treasures that were left by the
King...
Although we still love him and wish he were alive...
It's now become the King's tomb with his soul
trapped inside.

"Elvis and his mother had a special relationship. I think they shared the same dreams." -Anonymous

They shared a special language only they could
understand…
They had a special bond that no one could
understand…
He was her precious gift from God to share with the
world…
No matter what time of day or where he was…
He could always call his momma with his fears and his
sorrows…
They often talked about Jessie and wondered where he
was…
They had a special kind of bond that no one could
understand.

"People didn't like Jesus Christ and he was the perfect man." -Elvis

They tried to change him and make him look bad...
He always had the courage to stand up to them like a
man...
All throughout the years they never let him rest...
He always stood like a man and gave us his very
best...
He may have had problems and been in lots of pain...
He always came out to see us no matter what time of
day.

7-16-06

"If I could find any good hard rock songs I would record 'em." -Elvis

He was on top of the world at such a young age...
He had lots of gold records and money all around...
Although he was famous and known around the
world...
Something was missing inside and he still had not
found it...
Although he kept singing and making us laugh...
He lived a lonely life till he sang his last song.

"I was in tanks for some time ya see, and they Rock 'n' Roll quit a bit." -Elvis

Private Presley

He acted like a man and served his country proud...
He may have had a mansion and cars all around...
He made his country proud and served his time with
cameras all around...
Although he may have been gone to a foreign land...
He returned home proud and served his time for Uncle
Sam.

"I love seeing the pictures of Elvis from his last vacation; he was having fun and smiling. It's just too bad it was his last." -Anonymous

Last Vacation

During his last vacation on those Hawaiian islands...
The King of men saw something and turned towards
the sky...
It could have been the clouds; it may have been the
sun...
No matter what he might have found in the sky that
day...
Elvis Presley, the man, was called home and soon
found his way.

"I know Jessie Garon wasn't around but he was a part of Elvis' life that is sometimes over looked. I know Gladys believed that when one twin dies the other becomes a part of the one that didn't survive."
-Anonymous

America's King

America has made men into leaders and Presidents...
We've had some of the biggest entertainers in the world...
It's the place where a poor boy or girl can become a superstar...
America has had many legends and icons throughout the years...
America produced only one King and that man is Elvis...
America's King for all time.

"There was something special about Elvis, he didn't look like anybody else, or sound like anybody else. He was like nothing else I had ever seen." -Fan comment, 2007

Loves her father with all her heart...
Inspires us through her music...
Shares her feelings with us...
Admired for her spirit...

Made us cry with her music...
Adored and loved by many...
Remembers her father with love...
Incredible voice and soul...
Elvis loved her more than we'll know.

5-18-07

"The only thing I could say besides Jesus Christ, there's no greater man that ever lived in any respect, in loving his friends, in loving the world, in giving to the world. There's no way to express it, besides Jesus Christ he's the greatest man I ever knew." -J.D. Sumner, 1977

Aloha from Hawaii

Never had we seen an entertainer through a satellite…
Aloha from Hawaii beamed to over one billion live…
The first time in history our planet watched an entertainer live…
Elvis stood there on stage and let the Red, White and Blue shine…
Elvis' greatest moment was seen by one billion live.

"He truly loved giving to people. He loved to see that look on your face. That made his day." -Larry Geller

How can a man give so unselfishly…
Year after year, always giving something to someone…
No matter who you were or where you came from…
He loved to help his fellow man along the way…
Giving to those he knew best, and to those who he had never met…
He truly loved life and the people that were in it…
Even though you've been gone for thirty years now…
We miss you so much Elvis, and wish you were still with us.

"I never had the chance to meet Elvis but if I could go back in time, I would just tell him how much he was loved and how important he was to us." -Mike

Elvis…
We loved you in the beginning and we loved you till the end…
Elvis…
You gave us love in so many ways; it will take two lifetimes to pay you back…
Elvis…
You entertained us like no one else had, or since that day the music died…
Elvis…
You are the King of Music and will be for all time…
Elvis…
You had the most beautiful voice and no one can compare…
Elvis…
Since the day you left our world, it's never been the same.

"Although Graceland is the second most visited place in America, she will always be number one in the heart of an Elvis fan." -Mike

Graceland

A beautiful home without a heart...
She stands there for the world to see...
Although we travel there each year to give her a dose
of life...
She stands there lonely with no King in her sight...
The house may be filled with souls everyday...
She cries out for the soul that saved her life...

Although his tomb is there for all the world to see...
Maybe it's time we slow down and give the King his
privacy...
Although the gates are open for us to come inside...
Graceland needs some time alone to mourn the passing
of her King...
Even though we truly love him like a mother loves her
child...
I feel we need to slow down and let Elvis get some
rest...

 She stands there like a castle with no King at her
throne...
She sits and waits hoping one day he'll return home...
Although her soul is empty she did her best to save the
King...

So please don't forget Graceland as you go to mourn the King.

Elvis, Through My Eyes

When you ask an Elvis fan, "what is it that you love about him?" It's hard to put it into words because it's not just one thing. He embodied the essence of so many wonderful things we can never really find the words to describe him. For some it may be his looks, for others it may be his personality or the way he conveyed so many feelings through his singing. I'm sure for a lot of us it's all of those qualities and much more.

When I look into his eyes, I feel a connection to something more than just the person. It was like looking into an open window that led you into another world. At times he had the eyes of an innocent child, looking for something he couldn't seem to find. At other times, his eyes looked so sad that you couldn't help but wonder what he was thinking and feeling.

His personality was so incredible that he left an impression on every person he met. The women fell in love with him, and men wanted to be like him.

Even to this day, no entertainer has the charisma or natural charm Elvis did. When you watch him or listen to him sing, you can't help but be attracted to his voice and personality.

Another reason why people were so drawn to him was of course, his looks. He looked so different from everyone at the time; you couldn't help but notice it. He almost looked like he was from another place and time that we still haven't found. Other performers were inspired to become musicians because of the way he looked and performed on stage.

He truly loved giving to his family, friends, and people he had never met. To this day I don't know of a person who loves to give as much as he did. Not only giving money, but giving time to his fans and letting them be a part of his life. A lot of people don't understand how generous he was. It didn't matter to him if you were a movie star or a mechanic, he would stop and talk to everyone along the way. He loved his fans and made sure they knew how much he appreciated their love and support.

He had the most amazing voice I've ever heard. One thing no one can take away from Elvis was his incredible ability to express feelings through a song. He could sing anything and do it like no one else. He had a special way of singing a song that made each person feel as if he were singing to them alone. For a lot of fans, his music is our way to stay connected to him even though he's no longer with us.

You will never find a more loyal group of people than Elvis' fans. They loved him back then and have passed down that love to their children and family members. We all share the feelings mentioned in this book along with many other feelings we have in our heart. No matter where you are or where you go, by being an Elvis fan you know that you will always have a second family. Elvis was one of a kind, and will forever be remembered as the King.

The day Elvis died, the world changed and has never been the same. We lost a part of ourselves the day the music died.

Graceland Through My Eyes

I'm driving the 3000 miles to Graceland and I start thinking about this mythical place in my mind. Sure, I've seen pictures of this place a million times, but I had to see it for myself. I had exactly one week to get from California to Memphis, see Graceland and return home. Sure, you don't think it's much time, but when you are going to get to see where the King lived, believe me, it's worth it. We left on a Monday morning and arrived in Memphis Tuesday night. I couldn't even go to the hotel first; I wanted the dream to become a reality.

I pulled up in front of the wall and see a house that appears to be illuminated from the heavens above. I've seen pictures of the house hundreds of times but nothing compares to seeing it for the first time. At first, I was taken back in time and was a fan standing in front of the gates, waiting for a glimpse of the King. All too soon, I'm transferred back to the present and realize that He's not going to come out the front door. I'm saddened by that truth. I stood in front of the wall with tears running down my face.

The next morning I returned and stood in front of the wall and read what so many had written. You will never in your life see so many kind words about a human being. You don't want to ruin something that belonged to Elvis but you are compelled to leave your mark and just hope that when you return, it will still be there. It's a slow process getting tickets, but maybe I'm just in a rush to see the inside of where the King called home. I'm on the tour bus and I say to myself 'are we there yet' and that's just when we are crossing the street to get into the gates of Graceland. As soon as they open, I imagine the King driving through these gates with screaming fans all around. Finally, I make it to the front of the house and get to walk through the doors where Elvis himself walked through.

The pictures and video that I've seen of this house don't do it justice. Everything is so beautiful and it feels like Elvis is going to walk down the stairs and greet you any second. I felt his presence while walking through the house, like he was taking me on a personal tour.

Before I know it, I'm at the meditation garden. The inside of the house seems like a blur since I was in a hurry to get to where the King rested. It's sad seeing where his body lies and you hope that he's no longer in any pain where he is and that he has found the peace that he searched for in life.

Once you walk past his tomb, you want nothing more than to go back inside to see what you missed. When you get back in, you see everything this man had accomplished while he was alive. There was recognition from charities, Grammy awards, gold records, millions of other things that blow you away. Then you come back to the meditation garden and again I'm saddened by the fact that I never got to meet this legend.

I walk slowly away and before I know it, it's time to leave Memphis. The mythical place that was there before, returned in my mind and what I saw doesn't seem real anymore. Life goes on and the stories I heard will always be with me but time in Graceland stands still waiting for her master to return.

Facts about the King

Vernon and Gladys were married in June of 1933.

Elvis was born January 8, 1935 to Vernon and Gladys in a house that was built by his father and grandfather in Tupelo, Mississippi. Elvis was second of the two twins, born 35 minutes later. Jessie Garon was stillborn.

Elvis received his first guitar at the age of 11.

Elvis sings Old Shep at the Mississippi Fair in 1945 and takes home second place.

The family moved to Memphis in 1948.

Worked part time as a movie usher at Lowe's movie theater in 1952.

Elvis graduated from L.C. Humes High in 1953.

After Elvis graduated he went to Sun Records and paid the four dollar fee to record 'My Happiness' along with 'That's When Your Heartache Begins"

In the summer of 1954, Elvis was paired with too musicians, guitar player, Scotty Moore and bass player Bill Black.

July 5, 1954 was the night they stumbled upon Arthur Crudup's, 'That's All Right Mama' while messing around.

The flip side of 'That's All Right Mama' was 'Blue Moon of Kentucky'.

Elvis recorded five singles for sun records.

Elvis' first appearance on the Louisiana Hayride came October 16, 1954.

In November of 1955 RCA buys Elvis' contract from Sun records for the amount of $40,000.

In January of 1956 RCA released 'Heart Break Hotel' and it sells 300,000 copies in one week.

In January of 1956 Elvis performs in Jacksonville, Florida and is taken away to the emergency room after he collapses.

In March of 1956 Elvis' first album is released, it sells over one million copies.

In April of 1956 Elvis signs a seven year movie contract with Hal Wallis.

July of 1956 Elvis performs on the Steve Allen show and sings 'Hound Dog' to a Basset hound on stage.

Early 1956 Elvis performs in Florida, and only moves his pinky as he sings.

Elvis appeared on The Ed Sullivan show 3 times from September 1956 to January 1957. Elvis' last performance is filmed from the waist up.

'Love me Tender', Elvis' first movie, premiered in November of 1956.

Elvis purchased Graceland in March of 1957 for the amount of $102,500.

In December of 1957 Elvis received a Draft notice.

He is inducted into the army in March of 1958, he was stationed in Texas for six months of training. The registration number he was given was 53310761.

On August 14, 1958 his beloved mother Gladys passed away.

He made it home in time to see her before she passed away.

In September of 1958, Elvis leaves for Germany and is stationed there for 18 months.

Elvis met Priscilla in November of 1959 while stationed in Germany.

Elvis is promoted to sergeant in 1960.

Elvis returned home March 2, 1960.

On March 21, 1960, Elvis received his first degree black belt, and would later reach 8th degree black belt before he passed away.

Frank Sinatra's special, 'Welcome Home Elvis' aired May 8, 1960. Elvis received a fee of $125,000.

On March 25, 1961 Elvis performs at a fund raising concert for the U.S.S. Arizona memorial and raises over $65,000 for the project. This prompted others to donate and the memorial was completed a short time later.

The fund raising event is his last live concert until 1968.

From 1961 to 1968 Elvis is kept busy with his movie filming schedule.

December of 1966 Elvis proposes to Priscilla.

February 1967 he buys Circle G Ranch. It's a 163 acre ranch not far from Graceland.

May 1, 1967 Elvis and Priscilla become man and wife in Las Vegas Nevada.

February 1, 1968 Lisa Marie is born, exactly nine months to the day of there wedding.

Elvis begins filming in Burbank, for his first live performance since 1961. This special has come to be known as the '68 Comeback Special'.

Elvis returned to Memphis in early 1969 and records, four hit songs, 'Suspicious Minds', 'In the Ghetto', 'Kentucky Rain' and 'Don't cry Daddy'.

Elvis' comeback to live performing came in mid 1969 at the International Hotel.

He returns to the International Hotel in early 1970 to sold out shows.

Late February to early March of 1970, Elvis performs at the Houston, Astrodome. For six shows, he draws over 200,000 people.

In December of 1970, Elvis writes a letter to then President Nixon. Elvis meets with Nixon at the White House within hours of the letter being received by the President..

January of 1971 Elvis was awarded one of the ten most outstanding young men in America, By the United States Junior chamber of Commerce.

Speech Given by Elvis on that day...

Thank you very much ladies and gentlemen...

I'd like to thank the (Jaycees) for electing me as one of the outstanding young men...

When I was a child ladies and gentlemen I was a dreamer...

I read comic books and I was the hero of the comic book...

I saw movies, and I was the hero in the movie...So every dream that I ever dreamed has come true a hundred times...

These gentlemen over here, you see these type of people who care, are dedicated, you realize if it's not possible that they might be building the Kingdom of Heaven, it's not too farfetched from reality...

I'd like to say that, I learned very early in life...

Without a song, the day would never end...

Without a song a man ain't got a friend...

Without a song the road would never bend...

Without a song...

So I keep singing the song... Good night... Thank you.

June of 1971, a stretch of highway 51 that runs along Graceland is renamed Elvis Presley Boulevard.

Mid 1971, Elvis returns to the International hotel, now known as the Las Vegas Hilton. He plays to sold out shows once again.

In the beginning of 1972, Elvis goes on tour as he's filmed for the concert documentary, Elvis on Tour. This film won a golden globe award for best documentary.

June of 1972 marks the first time Elvis performs in New York at Madison Square Garden. The four shows were sold out attracting 80,000. Celebrities on hand included, Bob Dylan, John Lennon, David Bowie, among many others.

Priscilla files the papers for divorce in July of 1972.

January of 1973, Elvis is seen by over one billion as he performs from Honolulu Hawaii. This was the first time in history an entertainer was viewed by over one billion people. The album from this performance went straight to number one. This performance was seen in more American households than mans first walk on the moon.

In March of 1973 Elvis' catalogue of music is sold back to RCA for a sum of five million dollars.

October of 1973 the divorce is finalized in Santa Monica, California.

Elvis went back into the Memphis hospital in late October.

Mid 1974, Elvis was offered a supporting role in the remake of 'A Star is Born'. The Colonel tells Elvis not to accept the role because he would not be getting the lead role. Getting this part might have given Elvis a new lease on life, and a chance to be in a serious acting role.

December of 1975, Elvis performs in Pontiac, Michigan, setting a new attendance record of over 62,000 at a single show.

Early 1976, Elvis records an album from Graceland known as 'From Elvis Presley Blvd'.

Elvis goes on tour on and off from March till October of 1976.

December 31, 1976, Elvis performs on New Year's Eve to a sold out crowd in Pittsburgh, Pennsylvania.

Elvis hits the road again in early 1977 and is hospitalized due to fatigue.

In June, Elvis is taped for a CBS special to be aired, but the special never makes it to T.V. until after his death.

June 26, 1977 Elvis performed his last concert at the Market Square Arena, in Indiana.

Elvis is found dead in his home On August 16, 1977, passing away from heart failure.

Although he performed only half of the year in 1977, he outsold all other performers.

Thousands of people made their way to Graceland, hoping to get a final glimpse of their fallen hero.

Concert Attendance – 1969-1977

I have done my best to give you estimates on the number of people who attended Elvis' concerts between 1969 and 1977. After researching and finding what I could of the attendance records, over 6.1 million people attended his concerts. These numbers do not include the Lake Tahoe performances.

Over his lifetime, Elvis had been viewed on television by over 2 billion, that's right, I said BILLION, people worldwide. That estimate is from the time he started as an entertainer in the late 1950's until his death in 1977. That estimate is for his live performance's only; that does not include his movies.

No other entertainer had achieved such status as a single performer. During that time, remember that no one had cable or satellite television in their homes. All they had were basic channels. That's what separates Elvis from everyone else to this very day.

Here are some of the names Elvis had for his dogs and horses.

Dogs	Horses
Teddy Bear	Domino
Stuff	Rising Sun
Sweet Pea	Bear
Muffin	Colonel Midnight
Sherlock	Mare Ingram
Snoopy
Honey
Getlo
Fox Hugh
Brutus
Baba

Elvis Filmography

Film	Year
Love me Tender	1956
Jailhouse Rock	1957
Loving You	1957
King Creole	1958
Flaming Star	1960
G.I. Blues	1960
Blue Hawaii	1961
Wild in the Country	1961
Girls! Girls! Girls!	1962
Follow that Dream	1962
Kid Galahad	1962
Fun in Acapulco	1963
It happened at the World's Fair	1963
Kissin' Cousins	1963
Roustabout	1964
Viva Las Vegas	1964
Girl Happy	1965
Harum Scarum	1965
Paradise Hawaiian Style	1965
Tickle Me	1965
Frankie and Johnny	1966
Spinout	1966
Clambake	1967
Double Trouble	1967

Easy come Easy go	*1967*
Live a little Love a Little	*1968*
Speedway	*1968*
Stay Away Joe	*1968*
Charro!	*1969*
The Trouble with Girls	*1969*
Change of Habit	*1969*
Elvis "That's the Way It Is"	*1970*
Elvis on Tour	*1972*

My Favorite Portrayals of Elvis

Year	Actor	Title of Movie
1979	Kurt Russell	Elvis
1993	Val Kilmer	True Romance
1994	Peter Dobson	Forest Gump
1998	Harvey Keitel	Finding Graceland
2002	Bruce Campbell	Bubba-Ho-Tep

My Favorite Tribute Songs to Elvis

Cry Like Memphis by Tamara Walker

Walkin' in Memphis by Marc Cohn.

Black Velvet by Alannah Myles

Shine a Little Light On Elvis by Rex Fowler

Elvis Through the eyes of his fans

These comments were sent in to me by some of my online Elvis friends from all over the world.

The first time he came into my life was on that sad day he lost his life... Flaming Star was on TV....it was love at first sight...after the movie was over, I cried so much...because he died in that movie. And finally as the announcer said...Elvis Presley died in the hospital at the age of 42. I didn't stop crying till the next day, when mom came home from shopping and had with her, my first Elvis record. I've loved his music from that day on.....today I am 42 years old and I still love and adore him...and I will love him till the end of time. I adore him as a singer and actor. I think he is the most handsome and best looking man the world has ever seen. He is my best friend, a little bit like a father, (I don't have one), like a brother at other times. He is always on my mind and in my heart. When I am lonely I watch a movie or a concert on DVD....when I am sad I listen to his beautiful ballads and I feel better. When I am happy I dance and sing to his awesome Rock "n" Roll. He brought some wonderful new friends into my life. I think Elvis friends and fans are the best, nicest and truest group of people in this whole wide world.

If I ever get the chance to talk and tell Elvis my feelings I would tell him:

Elvis-thank you so much for being my friend, I was indescribably blue when you died.... you filled my life with love and joy. You are always on my mind...you are the King of my heart. Elvis, you are my endless love affair...and you mean the world to me...I will love you till the day I die.

Barbara, Germany

Elvis Presley for me is much more than just a good singer. My love for Elvis began since I was just a kid and it never faded away...Everytime I hear his heavenly voice it takes my breath away. He is my soul, a part of me .I feel so lucky to have known Elvis because he filled my life with so much happiness through the years, he is there for me every single day of my life and all I can do is just love him and spread that love with the world...No one can ever take his place he is just unique, in everything he did in everything he was.

Corina, Israel

How could one man mean so much, to so many, in so little time?

To think of what he accomplished! No one else has, or will ever, come close. To this day, he continues to make history. One can only hope to be half of what Elvis Presley was.

To listen to him sing, whether I'm happy or sad, will always put a smile on my face. Elvis Presley, we love you, we miss you, and thank you.

Karen Norman, Crown Point, Indiana

He was the greatest ever. He was almost not human like. When I listen to his music I get lost in it and it puts me in a happy place. Even when I am sad and I listen to the sad songs they put me at peace if only for the moment. Thank you Elvis.

Rick Puyallup, Washington

"Elvis, I will always luv ya...... Ya always seemed to be a part of my family".......,...... ~~~~ thanks, for the memories..... thank ya, thank ya very much........

Betty Jo, Houston, Texas

I will never forget Elvis, he will always live on in the hearts of his fans. There is something about Elvis that just makes you feel good, he is unforgettable. When my time comes to leave this earth I want to meet Jesus and then Elvis.

Cheryl, New York

He was a very thoughtful & caring person & he cared & loved all of his fans & family just as they loved him...He earned the name KING...& he became a Legend & the Legend still lives on...I'll always love his music & the way that he sang from his heart...He was truly blessed ...I thank God ...He blessed us with Elvis Aron Presley...TCB...

Shauni, Nevada

Elvis, Elvis, Elvis. What can I say? He is a one of a kind. There will never be another Elvis. He was, and still is the best singer today. There are people who can sing great, and perform great, but not like Elvis Presley. When I listen to Elvis, I get this special feeling. It is a great feeling. Only Elvis can do that, nobody else. I am a huge Elvis fan, and I will be for the rest of my life. Elvis will live on forever!!! ELVIS FOREVER!!!

Mike, Chicago

When I think about what Elvis "means" to me, of course my mind immediately goes to his voice, his good looks, his whole persona. But being an Elvis fan is much more than that to me. Elvis was a complex human being, human being the key word, because he was far from perfect. He had his faults just like the rest of us. I think that's what I love most about him - that he was human, not just the King of Rock and Roll, not just that persona. And despite the difficulties he had to deal with, he remained a warm, generous human being who cared for people deeply and genuinely.

Bobbi, Connecticut

Elvis I love you, I really do. Never regret what made you smile, and Elvis that person was you, and you still make me smile and always will. You are in my heart forever. You died but you live in me forever with your music, my love for you will never die. You are the King of my heart, and always will be, from your loving fan...

Valerie, United Kingdom

To me, Elvis Presley was and still is, the greatest performer who has ever lived in this world. His showmanship, magnetism, and his genuine love for his fans, earned him the name of "Evlis Presley, the King of Rock 'N Roll". Ever since I was a very young girl and heard him sing for the first time, I was already in love with him. Not only was he a fantastic performer but he was very handsome too! I will never forget him, nor will there ever be another one to take his place. When Elvis died, so did the music! I do want to thank all the ETAS for keeping his memory alive!

Gracie

California to Memphis

I made my way to the Promised Land of Memphis Tennessee by driving the 3000 miles to Graceland.

Birthplace of the King

The Lauder Dale courts where Elvis lived as a young boy

L.C. Humes High, Elvis' high school

Sun studios where Elvis recorded his first song

Elvis' first home on Audobon Drive

The passing of a King

Scatter, Elvis' chimpanzee

Beale Street

Memphis Tennessee

Here are various stadiums where Elvis performed, in no particular order.

Houston Astrodome in Texas, where Elvis performed to more then 200,000 people over his life.

Market Square Arena in Indiana, where Elvis performed for the very last time on June 26, 1977

Overton Park Shell founded in 1906, is where Elvis gave his first paid concert performance.

Madison Square Garden in New York, where Elvis performed to over 80,000 people during his performances there.

The Los Angeles Forum

Honolulu International Center, where Elvis performed the history making concert Aloha from Hawaii.

State Fair Coliseum, Jackson Mississippi.

Kansas City, Municipal Auditorium

Montgomery Garrett Coliseum

Shreveport, Hirsch Coliseum

Some of my favorite lines from movies in regards to Elvis...

How did you manage to slip through the 50's wearing
red velvet?
I slept.
Don't think you missed much.
Elvis?
Yes Elvis.

                    -Queen of the Damned

I thought I just saw Elvis,
Let it go Topper, the King is Gone.
                    -Hot Shots

I like you Clarence, Always have, always will.
                    -True Romance

Enough about the King, what about you?
                    -True Romance

Oh God, I hope they bring back Elvis.
                    -Independence Day

You do know Elvis is dead right?
No Elvis is not dead, he just went home.
                    -Men in Black

If that aircraft's carrying 30 prisoners, then I'm Elvis Presley.

-Con Air

Remember the King!

-Finding Graceland

What ever happened to Elvis?
He's uptown.

-The Heavenly Kid

You get in there with me, I'll take that shower.
-Bubba Ho-Tep

I added this last picture so that no matter where this book may travel, Our King Elvis, will always have the man he called the King looking over him.

I hope you have enjoyed reading these poems as much as I enjoyed writing them. There is one last thing I would like to say...

Remember the King!

www.ingramcontent.com/pod-product-compliance
Lightning Source LLC
La Vergne TN
LVHW011353080426
835511LV00005B/277